I0621092

My Life

Stefan, Born in Liverpool, Made in Colorado

Stefan Cairns, PhD.

Contents

About the Author

Other books by Stefan

Dentistry, and how it's damaging your health

Curing the Incurable

Life after Huggins

The Pharmaceutical truth

Insanity of man

Walk on through the wind
Walk on through the rain
Tho' your *Dreams* be tossed and blown
Walk on, Walk on, With *Hope* in your *Heart*
And you'll never walk alone
You'll never walk alone

University of Denver

Part One

Chapter 1: Preview

As I'm writing about my life to date, I obviously don't know what will happen in the future. I can make assumptions based on what I intend, and hopefully, I will achieve it.

But as we all know, life is extremely unpredictable, but... here goes.

Enjoy...

Southwell...

I suppose its best to start this book explaining where I am now. It's June 2024, and I'm living in a very nice Flat, or Apartment as it is referred to in the USA, where I lived for almost eleven years. More about that later.

Anyway, I'm not a spring chicken anymore, although even though I'll be 69 years old in three months, I still think of myself as I did when I was healthy and only forty-five.

The sad fact is that I was diagnosed with what is generally perceived to be an incurable disease, multiple sclerosis. As you can imagine, the disease, incurable or not, has drastically changed my life in a multitude of ways. I think the majority of sufferers of MS would naturally be saddened or even depressed to physically and emotionally lose what would be perceived as a very active life.

I'll explain a little of what I'm referring to. I've done 834 skydives; I was in the Guinness Book of Records in 1989, not for the number of jumps, because that's nothing in comparison to many skydivers I knew. No, it was because I was No. 2 on the 60-way formation accomplished at Sibson

Airfield in Cambridgeshire, near Peterborough. The record has been significantly beaten since, but back in 1989, relative work skydiving was in its infancy. I was also a Hang glider, Scuba diver, Rock climber Mountain biker, and I have my pilot's licence.

I'm digressing, sorry, so here I am, living on my own and spending the majority of time by myself, apart from three visits per day when my carers come, who obviously attend to things like my meal preparation or cleaning.

I don't get bored or depressed even though I probably only sleep three or four hours per day. Because the care workers are not allowed to physically help in any way, which I find absolutely ridiculous, I have a riser/recliner chair, as I couldn't sit up on my own in bed, so I wouldn't have been able to use a catheter while laying flat in my bed.

So I'm sat in my chair for twenty-three and a half hours seven days per week; I've only been out of my flat once in 18 months to visit a dentist. As I said, I dont get bored because I read a lot and write or research or watch TV. I know this situation would drive most people around the bend, but not me became I truly believe I will beat this freaking horrible life-sucking disease. How? That's for later, but for now, I'll outline the basics of my early life, which in reality is completely opposite to who and what I've become.

My Life-4

Chapter 2: Everton

It seems very strange, almost unbelievable, to me to come to terms with the fact that I was born in 1955. Obviously, the commonplace technology of today that's perfectly "normal" to kids these days wasn't even imagined, even by forward thinking individuals. It was very much a "black and white" world back then.

I was the third child born to my mum and dad, although mum had miscarried before and after me, which, looking back, explains the gaps.

Geoffrey, r.i.p. was born in 1950, Suzie (Susan then) 1951, me "55", Karen "58", Simon "60", Chris "61" and Brian in 1962.

So, seven kids living in a two-bedroom house, no bathroom, an outside toilet in the backyard. The only heating in the house was a small coal fire, which, as you can imagine, took an age to warm the room, let alone the house.

To us kids, it was perfectly normal to see the wall paper hanging off the bedroom wall as it was always cold and damp, especially in winter.

There were three rooms downstairs, although the middle room wasn't used per sè other than getting to the stairs or going into what we referred to as the "back kitchen". That room was a "dining room" although sitting at a little square table scoffing cornflakes in the summer months was the only "dining" that took place. There was a fireplace in there, but I don't remember a fire in there ever being on more than a few times over the twelve years I was there.

As I said, there was a little table and a couple of unmatched chairs. I remember bundles of laundry that had been dried on the clothes line in the backyard, then brought in and dumped in a pile.

Only "Sunday clothes" got ironed. I say "Sunday clothes" because it was almost a rule that everyone respected "Sunday"; most people wore their "Sunday best", shops were closed, and no paid work was done.

While we kids were out playing, mum would be doing the necessary jobs around the house. Being a family of nine meant laundry washing was a constant demand.

It's taken for granted these days to just quickly separate whites and colours and shove a load in the washing machine, then pop them in the dryer.

It was very different back then. A washing machine to us was a hulking machine that needed to be dragged next to the sink; two tubes were then attached to the taps, and the basic connections were useless, meaning they always leaked.

The drum holding the clothes just slowly alternated between turning one way and then the other.

There was no spinning involved. Fixed on top was a mangle of two rollers. They were just cylinders touching. When clothes were deemed washed, they would be fed between the contra-rotating cylinders, which squeezed the water out into the sink... hopefully. Then, weather prevailing, hung out to dry.

Before I was born, or at least just a baby, Mum was feeding the clothes into the mangle. Geoff thought this interesting, and while Mum concentrated on getting another shirt out of the washing drum, Geoff, who was standing on a chair, watching this amazing process, decided to put his finger into the mangle. Obviously, there were horrendous screams and panic as his hand was squeezed in, Mum desperately trying to turn it off and grab her 5-year-old, preventing further damage.

As I said, the world we know now was nothing like it was back then. Although he didn't lose his finger, then, he lost half of his index finger several years later.

Everton, a district in Liverpool, obviously had distinct differences. When looking at the residents, you were either a "Red" or a "Blue". At that time, the Blues were a dominant team and a true force to be reckoned with. The house we lived in, which in reality was a lot smaller than those seen on "Coronation St", was only about one mile from Goodison Park, the Everton stadium and another half mile from Anfield, so I'm sure you can imagine the number of supporters walking to their clubs on Saturday was in the thousands, very few people had cars. We learned at a very young age not to be "hanging around" on Saturdays if either team had lost. It was a normal thing to see gangs of lads wearing either a red or blue and white scarf prowling the little back streets looking for trouble.

I wasn't, nor have ever been, one of the thugs looking to fight just because they could. Obviously, Liverpool was a fairly rough place to live back then, so from a survival point of view, everyone had to learn to either be handy with their fists or just a good runner. Anyway, I made it this far, so I was obviously good at one or the other.

It seems completely alien to me to see kids preferring to spend the majority of their free time getting a neck ache, leaning over their smartphone, texting or chatting to their mate, often standing next to them instead of playing outside in the fresh air.

I remember being able to go to Woolton Woods with two or three mates to climb trees or just run around playing games. It was normal and I expected to get a good telling off because I'd stayed out longer than planned and was filthy, sweaty and had scuffed knees after my inevitable falls.

But, to get home and listen to the footy scores and see dad checking to see if he'd won on the football pools, which he never did, was still a comforting thing.

Mum would have been in the back kitchen, making what we referred to as "Tea" to us kids. Having our Tea meant the meal we'd have in the early evening, and "Dinner" was the meal at lunchtime.

As kids, we would laugh and think people were "posh" if they referred to "lunchtime" and evening "Dinner" back then. Very few houses even had bathrooms, and even fewer had gardens.

But in reality, I believe in my heart that I had a good childhood, even though we very rarely had special treats.

The Bombdies.

Being a kid, born only ten years after WW11 had ended, and living in a city which at that time was one of the major sea ports in England, it had obviously been heavily bombed by the German

Luftwaffe, resulting in areas that were unsafe and should have been avoided.

Not far from where I lived were houses, even streets that had been bombed and were planned to be demolished and rebuilt at some point, but to me and my mates, they were a great place to play. These were never known as "such and such streets". It was simply "The Bombdies ".

As little, boisterous kids, full of energy, we'd play by climbing all over the bombed house and play war games, chucking stones and half bricks at each other, getting "wounded" by having been hit my a stone, meaning you were obviously restricted in what you could do, the other army would win when a "soldier" had been directly hit by a bullet (stone) or hand grenade (half brick) and was forced to play dead by lying face down in the dirt and rubble.

My Life-13

For some unbeknownst reason (joke), I remember having to be taken to Alder Hey Hospital on numerous occasions because my head had been the final stopping point of a brick, resulting in a nasty cut and lots of blood running down my face. I think the nurses all knew me by name because of my frequent visits.

But as I said, as kids, it was all just good fun. We never actually thought about the possible consequences of falling though the floor, as my elder brother Geoff did once; fortunately, he didn't break his leg, and from our point of view, Jimmy, Vincent and myself just laughed.

Back then, kids didn't have any way to know, specifically what time it was; we just based it on the rumbling in our tummies, and we'd sheepishly approach what we thought of as an "oldie" and politely ask if they knew the time.

Upon hearing it was about a quarter past five, we'd panic and knew we'd have to "leg it" home in time for "tea", which, if we were lucky, would be "chips, beans, and sausage, and not a bowl of "scouse."

It's strange because back then, a bowl of "scouse", a stew made from chuck steak, lamb mince, carrots, onion and spuds (potato), wasn't considered a nice thing to eat, but, later in life, away from the very limited life I had, a bowl of scouse was great.

I know that the technological advancements over the last twenty-five years or so have been quite remarkable, actually incredible, these days it's become almost commonplace to hear or see on one media outlet or another that a new device or app is available to enable the "common man" to do things that would previously, have only been possible by specialists with access to equipment costing hundreds of thousands.

Completely different...

Back then, to us kids, at least, money was very different in so many ways.

Obviously, coins and paper money were the main form of currency. Looking back, the coinage was constantly being used or even just rattled in a man's pocket.

I'm sure it would be hard to imagine for "today's kids", but back then, there were eight different coins. I'll explain:

Farthing... this was a quarter of a penny.

Halfpenny... or half of a penny.

Penny... one-twelfth of a Shilling

These three were known as "coppers."

Three penny piece... or as we knew it, Thrupenny bit, had twelve edges.

Sixpence.. or a "Tanner" to those lucky to ever see it and was small and almost all silver.

Shilling... equivalent to 12 pennies. This was also silver.

Florin... known as a 2 Bob bit... equivalent of 24 pennies.

Half crown... equivalent to 30 pennies, and was silver and huge to kids.

We then jumped up to paper notes.

Ten shilling note... known as a 10 Bob note, was brown in colour and the equivalent of a half pound.

One pound note... was greenish in colour and rarely seen by kids like me.

But in today's world of smartphones and the thousands of instantly downloadable applications, information is available in the time it takes to type the question into Google.

That being said, it still shocks and frustrates me to see kids with their heads bowed while clutching their smartphones, chatting to their friends instead of genuinely talking to them.

As a kid, every chance I had to go outside and play was always snapped up. To me, being able to actually have a football and to play "footy" with my mates, Jimmy and Vincent, was great fun. Before we kicked the ball, we'd all assume the name of our favourite player and be yelling things like, Yeah, Roger Hunt just scored another goal, or "hey, good cross, Ian St John", and "Shankley will be proud of you".

Life as a kid back then was good; we were taught to be respectful of all adults, regardless of their financial standing.

The fact that the person talking was an adult meant that we looked at them and answered their question, unlike today, where a child can choose to ignore and be rude because they are chatting to someone online, and in their opinion, that takes priority.

I have to take a breath now rather than letting my frustrations with the unruly kids of today dominate my memories.

Looking back at the "everyday necessities" from a kids point of view, earning some extra pennies was quite important as getting a "tanner" for pocket money each week, if we were lucky, wasn't much, so we would all "run message's" for the older neighbours that didn't have kids.

To "run a message" meant to be given a few silver coins wrapped in a bit of paper with a message for the shopkeeper, telling him what was needed. Upon receipt of the food, we'd run back and hand it back along with any "change".

If I could run three or four messages each week, it meant earning enough to treat myself to something like a "Raspberry Ruffle" or a "Bounty", which at that time was absolutely amazing.

I don't know the specifics exactly of what my dad earned driving a truck delivering newspapers to lots of shops at night as far away as Chester in North Wales, but I do know it wasn't a lot and life financially, was very difficult.

I have many memories of being told to keep quiet when there was a debt collector banging on the door and days when I saw Mum standing in the corner, hiding her face because she was crying, knowing there wasn't enough money to pay the rent or buy food or to put a silver coin in the electric meter, meaning there would be no lights on at night.

My family— mum, dad and seven kids lived in that two-bed house in Everton till the late 60's. As a kid with no experience of nice and more comfortable surroundings, we just accepted the life we had and were always grateful for the rare treat. But in reality, I feel that when looking back, we had a great childhood, and for that and the many sacrifices mum and dad obviously made, I am truly grateful.

Chapter 3: Halewood

In the late 60s, Halewood was right on the outskirts of the Liverpool I knew. Here, there were lots of open fields and houses, still terraced but much bigger.

I think all of us felt as if we could be considered "Posh" as not only did we have four bedrooms and a bathroom... shock and amazement…but we even had a garden, it might have only been twenty feet square, but it was a garden, at that time, having spent the twelve or thirteen years I'd been alive, living in a two-bedroom house with an outside loo, was freaking amazing.

I mentioned earlier about going to "Woolton Woods". This was something we did on occasion after we'd moved to Halewwod, not when we lived in Everton.

Living here was literally a different way of life, moving house, in a completely different neighbourhood, changing schools and getting to make new friends, was, I'm sure you can imagine, to be quite an exciting challenge for all of us, well from Karen who was about eight yrs old, me, Susie and Geoff, obviously not so much for Simon, Chris and Brian who would only have been 6, 5 and 4.

It's strange, but the only thing that comes to mind about my school is that it was called Halewood Comprehensive. Back then, everyone walked to school, regardless of how far away it was.

My very first girlfriend, Gaynor Highfield, lived about 50 yards away on the other side of the street.

She was the very first girl I kissed. To kids back then, having a girlfriend wasn't considered a "boyish" thing to be proud of, and admitting a kiss had actually happened was not to be spoken of.

My new "best friends" lived in the end terraced house over the road. Colin and David were born just before and after me by a year. I didn't favour one or the other. We all just played the rough and ready games that kids our age did, running around, kicking footballs and climbing walls wherever possible.

Dad had become a bus driver. He didn't work the night shift anymore, which was obviously much better for him. In his previous job, he'd been a night shift driver for seven years, working six nights per week. The employment laws were non-existent then, meaning, regardless of how bad the working conditions and requirements were, you either took the job or you didn't. There were no rules in place at that time to ensure that working conditions were biased towards an employee.

As I said, the hours Dad worked we're definitely better, but the pressures on Mum and Dad to provide for the family they had created were even greater. From a financial standpoint, the requirements needed to move house, more rooms and furniture, etc.

The emotional challenges obviously created problems that we as kids were not fully aware of, but I know that Mum was very unhappy, so much so that she planned to break up with Dad.

Dad's older brother, Uncle Jim, who was obviously very unhappy in his marriage, decided to run away with Mum, as they felt the same. I could make assumptions as to their mindset, but in reality, only they themselves knew the specifics, so it would be unfair for me to condemn either for their actions.

Initially, Mum left for about a week or so and then came back. The second time was emotionally more challenging for us all, especially as my sister Sue, as she was then, also went for a day or two.

Dad had a plan which I was to play an integral part of. The plan was as follows: I was to say that Uncle Jim had come to the house to get some additional things for mum. He wasn't aware that I'd been off school and actually in the house, upstairs in my bedroom. I was to say that while Uncle Jim was rummaging through the clothes in the wardrobe, he found the old tobacco tin that dad used to keep the small amount of money he'd saved. I was to say I'd seen Uncle Jim open it and counted about £40, then put the tin in his pocket and grab the clothes for mum before leaving.

Now, remember that this didn't actually happen. It was just what I was to tell the police. This was Dad's idea to get Mum back and away from what he perceived as his evil big brother.

Sadly, there was a completely different chain of events. Normally, dad, Susie and I would have been up at about 07.30, getting things ready for breakfast and school, etc., but on this day, I woke and realised that there was no movement in the house, so I got out of bed then rushed in to make sure that dad was up.

Dad was a big man because of his eighteen years in the army, most of which had been serving in parts of Asia and Africa. He had what we thought of as a weathered tan. His face, neck and hands always seemed to be slightly tanned, not dark but not the sickly white of most people. Upon entering his bedroom, I could see dad laying on his back, his eyes open and staring at the ceiling. As a fourteen-year-old, I didn't know or didn't want to accept what I was seeing. I put both hands on his chest and shook him, saying, "Dad, Dad, you've overslept, come on, wake up". I must have tried waking him for a minute or two before I held his right hand while dropping onto my knees and crying as I realised he was dead. I took a deep breath, stood up and placed his hand beside his lifeless body. I went into Susie's room and woke her up. As she opened her eyes, I said, "Dad's dead" She jumped up and ran into Dad's room. The strange thing is that all she remembers is seeing Dad, not the part of me waking her up, so her memory is that she found Dad dead.

My Life-28

While she was crying, I went outside, and Mr Todd, a friend of dad, was just leaving for work. I ran over to him, and in a panicking child's way, I told him that Dad was dead. He told me to run to the police station, which was only about a half mile away, and to tell them what had happened.

I ran as fast as I could and burst through the door, shouting that my dad was dead. The desk sergeant came out to calm me down and take some details. After explaining who I was, etc, they put me into the back seat of a Police car and drove me to my house, 27 Antons Rd. I'll never forget that. The next hour was very much a blur, but I do remember the paramedics carrying Dad strapped onto a wheelchair down the steep flight of stairs and out to the ambulance. I also remember that Susie was gripping my arm and crying.

I'm not sure exactly how it happened, but a little later, mum and uncle Jim arrived. Obviously, I didn't know the whole story and the true reasons why mum had left, but from my teenage point of view, she had left us, and all I could see was someone that didn't love us, so I stood at the door attempting to prevent either coming in. Anyway after a few minutes talking, mum came in and comforted her children. I distinctly remember grabbing a big carving knife and then going into the utility room, where it was dark, as there were no windows. I held the point against my stomach, after I'd found Dad dead, I didn't want to live anymore. It was a stupid and ridiculous teenage thing to do. Needless to say, logic and true reasoning eventually took control of my mind, and I returned to the rest of my family, attempting to come to terms with what had happened and what was to happen.

Over the next few days, Mum moved back in and explained her reasons behind the move. I know dad was very much a disciplinarian, all of us, regardless of age, not the three little ones, but Karen, me, Suzie and Geoff, as kids, would get a spanked backside or cuff at the back of our head when we had done or said something stupid.

I haven't mentioned Geoff very much because he was working as an apprentice Carpenter. He still lived at home but had gone to work before Dad was found dead by me.

Fred...

I can't remember exactly, but shortly after, Mum and Uncle Jim were officially together as far as we kids were concerned. Being in the house where

Dad lived, from Mum and Uncle Jim's point of view, just didn't work so it was agreed another move had to happen.

Litherland, another district of Liverpool, was our destination. The main road running through Litherland was Linacre Rd, a major bus route adjoining Bootle, another rough place to live. It's strange, but every lamppost in Bootle was painted red from the ground up to about 10 ft, so you always knew if you were in or out of Bootle.

Chapter 4: Litherland

The second-hand shop

As I said, we were now living on Linacre Rd. Uncle Jim and Mum had opened what was a combination of Antiques and secondhand goods. We were at one end of four shops. I think it was a butcher's shop that was next door, and I remember a woman's clothes shop that was double-fronted next door to a newsagent at the other end.

I was now going to Litherland High School, a rather grandiose title for a school full of kids not wanting to genuinely learn, broaden their minds and have a better education. It was a regular monthly thing to arrange mass fights with another school that was a couple of miles away called Warwick Bolum, 30 or 40 kids would meet a similar number from Litherland High on a big patch of wasteland, and then a mass brawl would happen until it was broken up by police, who, on several occasions had luckily appeared before anything serious happened, instead of resulting in outcomes common in video games watched and played by the moronic kids of today that have had their minds twisted by video games dominated with mindless violence and death. In the weeks prior to "the fight", one of the main instigators, a knuckle-dragging thug known as "Monk", would be threatening any kids, like me, not wanting to attend.

Another problem I faced at this particular school was that most classes had one or two bullies, which created a very distinct level of fear among anyone who genuinely wanted to improve their knowledge and education. I wasn't what you would consider a "brainiac", but I definitely wanted to learn a little more than what appeared to be the norm for a lot of other kids. This resulted in beatings by some of the knuckle draggers and days that I'd leave school early.

One of the good things that happened was the relationship between myself and Uncle Jim. He would never replace my dad, obviously, but a friendship was developing unlike any I'd had before. He taught me so much about antiques and coins I'd often accompany him to auction rooms and get a better understanding of the good sellers that, in reality, helped us as a family live a better life. I refused to call him Jim, as he'd suggested. He was my uncle, yes we'd become friends, but he was an adult, and I was only fifteen, so we agreed that I call him "Fred" I don't remember where that came from, but the name "Fred" seemed to be used by everyone, no-one called out for "Uncle Jim" it was always "Fred".

The house was basically the shop front on Linacre Rd, and the street to the side was "Violet Street," behind the shop was the kitchen used by the family, then a small utility room and the back door leading to the high walled backyard.

As I said, this wasn't what you'd think of as a nice area of Liverpool. In fact, on top of the high brick walls was cement with broken glass bottles sticking up as a deterrent to burglars.

Alongside the kitchen was the flight of stairs leading to the family living area.

A big living room, a bedroom and a bathroom were on this level. Another staircase led to three more bedrooms, one of which was sandwiched between the front and back. This room only had a "skylight" on the roof. This was where Geoff and I slept in bunk beds. Geoff r.i.p. was never what I'd consider a good brother. He always had smelly feet and insisted on making his little brother, me smell them.

Geoff was different from the rest of us. Maybe it was because he was the eldest, although he didn't actually help Mum and Fred. I remember that he always had really smelly feet that he insisted on sticking right in front of our faces whenever possible. As we all grew older, I think we all saw him in a different light, back then he wasn't liked by any of his siblings, but as an adult, Geoff was a nice, generous and considerate man, and we were all deeply moved and saddened by his passing shortly after his 60th birthday... r.i.p.

I think, looking back to the time in Litherland with Mum and Fred, it was a time that I genuinely believe I learned so much about life and realised that I had to look further afield if I was to make something positive happen in my life, so, I looked at joining the army as a boy soldier.

I remember mum and Fred taking me to the city to get to the Army recruitment office.

Sitting down with what appeared to be a very understanding and motivational sergeant filled me with inspiration and the desire to genuinely further my education and learn a trade while also understanding the discipline needed to succeed in life.

So, I signed on the dotted line to attend a military college.

It was about three months later that I would be leaving home. Yes, it was exciting, but I was also very nervous about it. I was only fifteen years old and had made a commitment to leave home and attend a military college 150 miles away. In the back of my mind, I was thinking, "WHAT HAVE I DONE?".

I remember mum and Fred getting a nice suit for me, which was completely opposite to how I was normally dressed. The last time I'd worn smart clothes like this was probably five years ago on Sundays in Everton, and I definitely felt that it just wasn't me and as if I was standing out like a sore thumb.

Fred wanted me to not just look smart but also to have a really good suitcase. Back then, people didn't have many options. It was either a nice, expensive case or a cheap one. Fred, through the shop, had bought an upmarket case called a "Revelation"... this was a really nice case, but slightly worn out and scuffed, but it had what was thought of as good and quite special expanding hinges, wow, at the time, I wasn't sure if having a posh suitcase was going to be a good thing or not.

As the day for me to leave home got closer, I remember feeling not just nervous but downright petrified. It's hard to genuinely relay the level of anxiety I felt. I was just a "kid", and other than a school trip to the Isle of Man several years before, I'd never left home and the protection of mum, but in a few days, I was genuinely leaving my safe place and going to what I expected to be a very disciplined military college, I knew that I'd seriously have to toughen up.

If I remember correctly, it was Tuesday, 4th May 1971, that I was taken to Lime St Station by Mum and Fred; going to the station, which was full of busy-looking adults, all walking fast or staring up at the big information signs showing the train times and relevant platform numbers. Although I was with Mum and Fred, I felt very much alone. I was trying hard not to show my fear, but I'm sure it was emanating out of me, and I know mum could tell.

I was only 4 ft, 11 inches tall, just a small kid, wearing a new suit and a tie, which I'd never done before. I was holding the big Revelation suitcase and about to get on a huge train. Mum hugged me after putting an envelope in my pocket. She was trying to hold back tears and whispered, "If you don't like it, you can always come home".

I knew that I couldn't cry as the train started to move and I saw Mum and Fred waving goodbye.

Chapter 5: Different Country

Although Wales is part of Great Britain, to this 4' 11" little boy, it felt like I was in a completely different country. I'd had to change trains at Birmingham New St and missed the connection, so by the time I'd arrived in Chepstow, everyone else had been through the initial recruitment and had already been installed into the relevant building for A, B or C company. This was decided upon by the trades we'd chosen to apprentice in. Mine was as a carpenter and joiner, so I was in B company. I was informed that the new me was Sapper Cairns and was part of the 71B intake. The total number of boys in all three Companies for that intake was about 120 or 130, meaning about 40 or so in each. Because I'd missed my connection in Birmingham, the other boys were all settled in and had already started making friends, so it felt really strange and a little scary being the last in and seeing the other boys already in their allocated bed space. Being only 4'11" meant I was the 3rd smallest. I'll always remember the littlest was a lad called Norman Fendyke, who was in the bed next to me.

The bed was next to a big metal closet and the clothes making up my new military uniform were all either hanging or folded.

All shirts, T-shirts, shorts and underwear were folded, not just haphazardly folded, but very specifically folded to the same width, exactly, and I mean exactly, not nearly or closely, but exactly to the millimetre and in specific groups.

The next morning, I remember feeling very shocked and insecure when I was being woken by the full corporal shouting and banging on the metal wardrobes.

After using the bathroom and getting dressed in my ill-fitting military uniform for the first time, we were taken to the "mess" to have breakfast. At this time, we were still unsure of exactly what and how things should be done, but that was all about to change.

Being asked to do something didn't happen. What we all very quickly learned was that the military staff all shouted instructions, we were all told what to do, and it had to be done exactly and immediately, no waiting or thinking, just doing.

Everything on that first day was all about understanding that discipline was first and foremost from now on.

In some ways, I was very lucky; having about 40 boys in 4 rooms and trying their best to adapt to this new life obviously had its problems. As I said,

I was the 3rd smallest and likely to be pushed around by the bigger kids, but the two biggest were on my side to a certain extent. One lad was from Manchester and wore braces on his jeans, and because of this he was always called "Granddad", the other biggest lad was Pete Cousins, they told everyone that because I was from Liverpool, I must be a hard case and not to be messed with, their warnings to the lads in my platoon definitely helped and meant that I didn't have to physically defend myself as frequently as I initially expected.

During the first week, trying my hardest to adapt to being in the army, yes it was a boys' college, but it was a military college, so all military rules and regulations had to be understood and adhered to; in fact, it was even more strict as we were all between the ages of fifteen to nineteen, so, children in the eyes of the law and even more so in a military college.

I think that the "Growing up" stage of my life was accentuated not just by being in the army and the strict rules and regulations that had to be adhered to but experiencing new and exciting things, which made this a very influential time in my life.

I'd managed to get a motor scooter, a Lambretta L.I. 125, which, in my opinion as a seventeen-year-old, made me feel like a proper "grown-up".

After one of my many weekend visits to Bristol to see my girlfriend, whose name escapes me, I was riding back to camp, obviously still being a learner and having the mandatory L plate stuck on the front and side. I wasn't allowed on the main carriageway on the Motorway over the Severn Bridge, but I could travel on the cycle path.

About halfway over, the scooter suddenly started to become totally unstable as my back tyre was punctured. I was lucky not to crash into the side barriers.

So, being halfway over the Severn Bridge at about 8.30 p.m. and knowing that I'd be in big trouble if I didn't report back to the Guardroom before 10 p.m. I left my scooter and started to run and pray I'd manage to get a lift, as there was no chance of running the ten miles or so in just over an hour.

What was so frustrating was that the Bridge crossed over the river Severn obviously, and the river Wye. Between the two was Beechley Head, which was home to my camp and where I needed to be.

Under sections of the bridge were motorised sections that were used for maintenance, etc. Access to them was restricted by angled barriers over the handrail, preventing easy access, but in my mind, climbing over and around this would enable me to get on the motorised carriage under the bridge. I wasn't thinking of the dangers and stupidity. I just needed to get to camp before 10 p.m. because I had always been an agile climber. I managed to wheedle my way around the angled barrier and down onto the carriageway.

It wasn't easy, but I opened the box with the controls and amazingly started the motors to move the carriage further along under the bridge and hopefully to a point where I'd be able to get down to the safe ground. I know now that it was a ridiculous thing to do, but hey, I was seventeen.

Fortunately for me, when the carriage reached the bridge support on the camp, although I was still about 30' above ground, a tree was very close, so the "I'm unbreakable" side of me decided that I could climb over the rail and jump into the tree.

Yes, I know it was a stupid thing, but after several nearly letting go attempts, I eventually leapt as if I was Spiderman. I crashed into the hard tree and clung to the branches; my weight on the skinny branch made it sag, and as it bowed, I then dropped down what I think was about 10' onto the ground; incredibly, I'd made it back to camp.

The excuse I made for my cuts, bruises and torn jacket was that I'd been mugged by two guys who stole my scooter.

The following day, the bridge security, the police and the military all took serious actions because, in 1972, there were still problems with the IRA, so although the bridge wasn't closed, only one lane in each direction was open for a couple of days, so yes, I felt bad-ish, but in my teenage mind, I'd done what was necessary regardless of the consequences.

A mate of mine took me to get one of those cans that re-inflated the tyre by squirting air and pressurising rubber into it.

Looking back, I realise that this was probably the most important part of my life. Being instructed in military discipline has had what I believe to be the best grounding in life. It wasn't just understanding "right from wrong" or respecting my elders, but it instilled the attitude to do it properly which I think is missing in so many people. I very quickly learned that if a job is worth doing, it should always be done properly.

Because I was one of seven kids, it had always been required to help out at home, but in this new environment where rules and regulations were in abundance and the necessity to always keep things clean, tidy and in order, took my views on life to an elevated level. Having this training as a boy made me into what I believe to be a better person who respected other people and, more importantly, myself.

None of us actually liked what we did, but we all knew it would be a time of our lives that we would all be proud of.

I'm sure that my natural competitive nature was enhanced simply by the fact that everyone was

My Life-51

encouraged and rewarded by always trying to do and be the best.

It really frustrates me to see so many teachers, instructors and even parents telling kids that competing isn't necessary.

The world is a far better place because of the competitive desires of so many people.

It's strange that even the "non-competitive" people will applaud and cheer the Olympians or Football teams for being the best, but they themselves wouldn't try hard or refuse to overindulge in eating tasty foods that are negatively harming their bodies.

Over the next three and a half years, I furthered my education and qualified as a carpenter and joiner. I had to pass my "City and Guilds", the civilian qualification, as well as the military "B2".

Although it seemed superfluous at the time, I continued my training, which meant that I took and passed my degree in Building Construction and Building Science.

After the boy service in military college, my first real posting was to the 41st company at Waterbeach near Cambridge. This was going to be another significant change in my life. I wasn't going to be in a military college with other boys/young men; now, I was going into the real army.

I can definitely say that although this was an exciting thing to be doing, I was crapping myself.

Chapter 6: Man-Service

Shortly after being informed that I was being posted to Waterbeach Camp, about 6 miles from Cambridge, I had a few days at home with family, and then I was to report to Waterbeach Camp and begin my Man-service.

This, again, was a very exciting time. I really did not know what to expect, but I did know it was going to be very different from being in an extremely strict military college.

I think being in an environment that was also very strict, but in a different way, was going to take a lot of getting used to.

I remember meeting a couple of fellow squaddies who were only a year or so older than me who befriended and guided me in the necessary basics of being in the man's army as opposed to colleges with other teenagers.

It was a very strange period of my life in that there were changes in my own perception of what actually mattered to me personally and how I wanted to move forward, ensuring good health, fitness and a genuine desire to improve myself physically and mentally.

One of the "good mates" I'd made was a guy who was either very much liked or very disliked because of his natural good looks and fitness. He seemed to have charisma and girls were very easily attracted to him, which made some other guys extremely envious, verging on not liking or trusting him. Maybe I was naive, but I got on with him really well, so much so that we were thought of as two best mates and always seen together after work. To a certain extent, he encouraged me to be stronger and fitter. Every year, we had to pass the FFR, the Fitness For Role test. Obviously, the guys that had administrative or "desk jobs" primarily weren't expected or required to compete with the physically active guys that could possibly be in a physically demanding military role but still do the FFR, as for me? I wanted to be the best, or at least be up there competing. I remember having to climb a 10' wall, then leap across a 6' water ditch, I had to carry a fellow squaddie over my shoulder, I think it was for about a hundred yards, then swap over, then complete a five-mile run, this was all done wearing "battle gear", to make it more like what could potentially happen in an extreme war-like environment. In the end, I was really pleased with myself in some ways because out of the four hundred competing that day, I finished in 7th place, which was definitely good, but the fact that my best mate finished in 4th sort of pissed me off.

Because I'd done well, I was told about the possibility of training to be a P.T.I. or Physical training instructor, which, at that time, very much appealed to me. I remember seeing them all looking so good in their P.T.I. gear, so I enrolled. What I didn't know or take into consideration was the level of commitment required. In reality, I was nowhere near being able to fulfil that role, and I feel quite embarrassed that I allowed other things to distract me instead of training hard. Looking back, my friendship with my best mate became too distracting. I wanted to go out, meet girls, drink beer and have a good time instead of focusing on genuine progression and improvement in life.

I was still a teenager and very easily influenced to indulge in what was pleasurable rather than what

I'd committed to. I'm actually embarrassed thinking about it now, and I remember sitting around one Sunday morning with a bunch of mates all talking about "life" One guy asked me what I thought I'd be doing when I was 50 years old. My head jerked back, and my eyes opened wide. I said, "Fifty.... 50 yrs old!!! I'll be dead by then. That's ancient". As I've said before, "Teenagers and Twenty nothings know didlysquat about what genuinely happens in life. I don't mean that as an insult because it's not. It's simply a statement of fact.

My Army career, limited as it was, definitely taught me a great deal of important things needed to survive in life. My only "Posting" in Man-service was at Waterbeach, but I did have several "exercises" to numerous places and saw and experienced a great deal.

It's weird thinking back and recalling how I thought and felt about my options when, in reality, I knew very little about life or what would happen in the future.

But as I said, I was still a teenager, and as all sensible adults know from experience, all teenagers know best, or at least that's what they think, and for me, a well-liked, athletic teen with a Suzuki 250 GT, I was going to enjoy my life, not waste time with crap like studying, I mean, I couldn't care less about what would happen when I was an old git of 40.

It's frightening to think about how the mind and perception of a teenager works.

Because my best mate had watched a movie called "Enter the Dragon" with Bruce Lee, we kept trying to mimic the moves, the inch punch and the high kicks, yes, stupid looking back, but at the time, it seemed like a cool thing to do.

One particular girl, a barmaid in the King's Head pub, thought I was a cool dude and let me know how she felt. So we started seeing each other, she was an Irish girl called Marie and lived in a flat on Mill Rd in Cambridge. I remember her so well, and the song "When will I see you again" by The Three Degrees will forever be a special song as it was playing when I lost my virginity to her.

Over the coming years, there weren't any life-changing experiences other than one particular act of stupidity that resulted in me and the army parting ways.

I have to make this clear and emphasise that, yes, I'd acted illegally and stupidly, but my actions never hurt or affected another person.

My Life-60

Chapter 7: Yorkshire

Leaving the Army definitely made me feel like a failure. I'd acted stupidly; it wasn't anything that created a problem from a civilian standpoint, but in the Army's eyes, a good mate and I were not to remain in military service. I am truly ashamed of my stupidity. I'm not going to even attempt to justify my actions. I was wrong and was punished appropriately.

Now what?

Fortunately for me, a couple who had become friends with my mum were kind enough to take me in as a lodger.

Les and Marjorie weren't actually married, although everyone, including me, thought they were.

Initially, I lived at home with Mum in Litherland, but shortly after Les and Marjorie had moved up to a small town in Yorkshire, I moved up there with them.

Now remember that I was born in Liverpool, I was stationed in South Wales, and then Waterbeach in Cambridgeshire. I obviously met a variety of people with different accents, but living in Yorkshire was a completely different experience.

Before I get into the differences, the unique attitude and stance of the everyday person, I have to say that I loved it!!!! Yes, it took a little while before I was accepted, but as soon as that

My Life-62

happened, I was one of what Yorkshire people perceive as "one of them" and, as such, trustworthy.

The small town that I lived in was famous for many things. Barnoldswick was in the Guinness Book of Records because it was the longest place name in England, that a letter wasn't repeated.

In and within a few miles of Barnoldswick, or "Barlick", as referred to by the locals, were four Rolls Royce factories that employed thousands. These factories were not for car manufacturing. No, this was where the turbine engines for aircraft were made.

The second famous fact, an engine that was used in several massive passenger aircraft, was the RB211.. or the Rolls Barnoldswick 211.

Just outside Barnoldswick was a tiny hamlet called Salterforth, known locally as "Soddam". This was also in the Guinness Book of Records because it had the shortest 30 mph speed limit in the country. If you were driving between Barnoldswick and Colne about 8 miles away, you'd encounter this change from 60mph to 30mph, then back to 60mph.

The distance between the sixty limits was about 35 yards or 30 metres. I think that over 50% of drivers ignored the change at their peril because I think there were at least 10 speeding tickets issued every week for non-locals.

Barnoldswick was also home to "Albert Hartley's", which at the time was one of the biggest textile printing factories in Europe.

Les Ellis was one of the "Chargehands" in the colour department, so again, I was very lucky to not only get a job but be specifically and properly trained in the making and perfecting the barrels of liquid used for printing the thousands of yards of material used by companies like Marks and Spencer.

It's strange but also quite flattering when I'd see curtains or sheets advertised in shops or in catalogues, and I knew that I'd been integral in their production.

During the first year or two, I worked on a three-shift rota, being on earlies, 6 am till 2 pm for a week, then 2 pm till 10 pm the next, then nights, 10 pm till 6 am was obviously good for "Hartley's" to have printing done 24 hours per day, but from my point of view it completely buggered my sleep cycle, I now understand what and why the

My Life-65

Circadian Rhythm is so important, but back then all I knew was that I hated three shifts.

So because of that and my training by Les and the senior colourist, I was promoted and able/responsible to only work the night shift, so now it was only four nights, Monday to Thursday, but I actually was paid more.

In reality, working the night shift was so much better for me and most of the other workers. I'd convinced everyone that having a permanent set of night shift workers meant that everyone else was only working a two-shift system.

Because of this, I was definitely thanked by just about everyone. The guys were happier, especially as they had less hassle to deal with at home, and my life in general was better. I only worked 4 nights, had more responsibility and had better pay.

My Life-66

I think that the discipline and other skills that had been instilled in me during my years in the army made a good impression on me and my employers.

Being in a better position financially definitely helped. I'd not only passed my motorcycle test but also my car driving test, but it was the bike side that appealed to me mostly at that time, so when the opportunity came up to get a big bike, I jumped at it.

A Suzuki 750cc water-cooled triple was a monster of a bike in the seventies. I'd been able to get a bank loan and get the bike, which not only looked good but sounded unique and so special.

Mum and Fred and the family had moved up from Liverpool to a village near Barnoldswick called Earby so I moved back in with mum.

I hadn't planned it, but it seemed that I had developed quite a reputation as a force to be reckoned with, not just because of what I'd done at Albert Hartley's but also because having the bike and how I rode it up and down a hilly and very twisty section of road, I've no idea if it had an official name, but locally it was known locally as "the wissic".

The Wissic was on the edge of Earby and started just beyond the much-frequented pub, The Beau Brummell" and wound uphill for about a half mile. I was known locally as "killer" because of my bike. The water-cooled triple made a unique sound when revved. I was also known as the mad scouser who rode the wissic faster than anyone else. It was not a good thing or things to be famous for locally, but in reality, I loved it.

Barnoldswick was also thought of by some people that it was in Yorkshire, but the fact is that when boundaries were moved in the 80s, it became part of the parish of Pendle in Lancashire, obviously because of the dislike of Lancashire by Yorkshire people. This was never accepted by the older generation.

Anyway, as far as I was concerned, it was a great place to live. It's a pity that I and a great many people simply didn't know of or appreciate the beautiful countryside.

Strangely enough, it's only about a 10-minute drive from Skipton, a beautiful market town, also famous for its 900-year-old castle and known as "The gateway to the Dales".

Living here, as I said, was very different in a multitude of ways. I had a complete change in attitude to life, and to respect the beauty of what surrounded me, I was living a stone's throw from The Dales.

For the unlucky people who, for whatever reason, have not witnessed the beauty of this incredible part of England, let me attempt to explain.

The total area that locals think of as "The Dales" is mainly in Yorkshire but also on the edges of Lancashire. The national park known as "The Dales: includes a section of "The Pennines", and trust me, it is beautiful.

It was here that I spent so much time hiking with a couple of mates as well as on my own. I think that at the time, I didn't appreciate how lucky I was. One particular day, I was "Rock climbing" with a friend called Jeff. I clearly remember the excitement I felt to be "free climbing" with no ropes, having only a chalk bag hanging off my belt.

Jeff, being a more experienced climber, would lead, leaving chalk handhold marks for me to follow. One particular weekend after it had rained the previous day, we shouldn't have, but we did attempt a small 30' climb, thinking that it would be an easy.... big mistake. The sound I heard as Jeff fell from about 20' and the sickly "THUD: when he hit the ground will forever be ingrained in my mind and remind me to always adhere to the correct procedures when doing anything, especially potentially dangerous sports.

Anyway, after a couple of minutes, because Jeff had landed face down on soft ground, he, fortunately, was still conscious and completely aware of what had happened. We both decided to take him to the hospital, so with his arm over my shoulder to support him, we limped the half mile back to his car. Being in such a remote area, it was a good 30 minutes before arriving at the hospital in Keighley. It was probably a 90-minute stay in the hospital before he was allowed to go home. Needless to say, our "Free climbing" adventures ended. Only "Roped" climbs ever happened for me, at least, although I don't know about Jeff.

I look back and remember that living in Barnoldswick, surrounded by Skipton, Burnley, Keighley and the beautiful countryside of the Dales, was at the time an under-appreciated experience, but I was only a young man, uneducated in the beauty of the northern countryside.

Cambridge...

For some unbeknownst reason in my memory, I'd started having a few long weekend trips back down south to Cambridge.

It was here that I met my first proper long-term girlfriend, who, in all fairness, changed so many things in my attitude and life in general.

Claire was different, she liked different music, and she rarely wore shoes, even on days that she had to nip out to a local shop. I think we dated for about two years, and I'd moved in with her. Well, actually, she was living in her grandmother's house in a small village about 25 miles from Cambridge.

I'd started working for a small building firm that took on a very wide variety of work.

One particular job was working for Cambridge Water Authority, where I met Juliet. She was one of the analysts analysing sewage, not an appealing job from my point of view, but obviously, one that interested her.

To cut a long story short, I was so enamoured by her that I ended it with Clair and moved in with the recently divorced Juliet, who lived in Cambridge.

Chapter 8: New Family

Looking back on my life, I can see very different chapters that have obviously made very distinct impressions on me and how I've behaved, some, like this next phase, which significantly influenced who I am.

Juliet was a year older and, as I said, was recently divorced. I was the complete opposite of her in that she was a very well-spoken, highly educated woman who had been raised as one of two daughters who, luckily, had never experienced the hardship I'd seen. I should have realised that I was an on the bounce mistake for her, but no, I was almost mesmerised by her beauty, intelligence and what appeared to be a carefree attitude.

In all honesty, her dad was unique in that he owned a steel components manufacturing business that he had built up from scratch. He was not averse to long working hours and genuinely deserved the benefits and financial rewards generated by his efforts.

What I loved about him was that he'd become a self-made wealthy man. He always made me laugh, seeing him with his hands engraved with oil and wearing his flat cap, getting into his one indulgence, a red Ferrari.

After dating Juliet for several months, which included weekly Sunday or whole weekend visits to spend with her family, don't get me wrong, I enjoyed seeing them, especially when her dad let me occasionally have short drives of his car, these were only ever for 5 or 10 miles on country roads away from any traffic, but I have to say, the exhilaration of driving a Ferrari Dino at speed along winding country roads was so special.

On the occasions that we'd gone for the weekend, Jim, her dad, would sit with me and have long talks. I never felt as if I was being interviewed or interrogated, although I was being plied with copious amounts of Macallan whisky.

On most occasions, the long weekend visits were enjoyable, but I genuinely felt that I needed something other than that. It became very obvious that Juliet was trying to change everything about me and convert me into one of the "Country sets" that she was more accustomed to. It just wasn't me to be wearing a flat cap, Barbour jacket and green Hunter wellies.

I was working as a sales executive in the I.T. industry for an american company with an office in

London. The company was involved in computer based typesetting and manufacturing seriously big printing press equipment.

I honestly felt a great deal of stress, firstly because Juliet constantly put pressure on me to earn more. We were now married and had a daughter, and I had taken on a big mortgage to live in a lovely house overlooking a marina in a Cambridgeshire village. Sounds good, I know, but as I said, the pressure on me to achieve, was getting me to the point of emotional exhaustion.

Secondly, coming to terms with the complexities of this new to me industry and now having to work primarily in the city of London was so mentally tiring. I was up at 5 a.m. to shower and get ready for work. I would leave at 6 a.m. and drive for two hours to get to my office at 8 a.m.

then I'd often be talking to customers on the phone or having meetings in the City.

At the end of my first full year, I won an award for being the top-selling "Newbie ". My prize was a holiday in Morocco.

It was a group trip. I seem to remember that six others, all senior and far more experienced than me, also went. I genuinely felt like a blessed and very privileged young man while in Marrakesh. One excursion was to Ouarzazate in the High Atlas Mountains, its difficult to genuinely explain the extremes of beauty and poverty I witnessed there.

A couple of years later, after being reasonably successful at what I did, I also became one of the top salesmen in the specialist field of what was then the new digital typesetting equipment and won another trip, this one was to Cairo in Egypt. I stayed in the hotel called "Mahmoodia Hotel" that Winston Churchill stayed in, I think, but in reality, it was a long time ago.

As a group of six, I believe we all rode camels in the Sahara Desert and had trips to the Pyramids. We even had unique trips into the center of the pyramid to the sarcophagus to see the burial tomb. I also saw the "Son et Lumière" light show, which was absolutely stunning. I was extremely lucky to have seen these things.

A year later, back at I.T. Graphix, where I worked, was obviously very rewarding, but having the constant daily pressure of my wife nagging me to earn more and the four hours driving to and from work, every day, which included two hours of dreaded M25, in all honesty, made me very weak emotionally, resulting in me, very wrongly and stupidly having an affair. It would be easy to try to justify, but morally, I was wrong regardless of my emotions.

Adrenaline junkie

One day, my brother Simon (one of five brothers) came to stay for a couple of days. He had just returned from Canada, where he'd been on exercise with the Army.

He took great pleasure, almost gloating that he had done a parachute jump. I'm sure that you can understand that because he is one of my younger brothers, there was no way on earth that I was going to let him have the satisfaction of beating me, so I did a thorough search and found that Peterborough Parachute Centre (PPC) was only 45 minutes away, and was on the phone to find out about training.

Apparently, a weekend course wasn't expensive, so I booked myself, Simon and Chris in for the course in two weeks' time.

There is obviously an emphasis on safety, so understanding exactly what, when and how to follow a very precise procedure would ensure that the exit from the plane and very specific position when landing would hopefully keep the student safe and broken leg free.

I very clearly remember the fear in the pit of my stomach as the aircraft climbed to altitude, and the eight students were huddled together in a specific position in the correct order to exit.

As the older of the three brothers, it was me that would be leaving the "jumpship" first. When the jumpmaster had given corrections on the direction to the pilot and the aircraft reached the appropriate altitude, and the jump master, Dave Morris, signalled for me to shuffle forward as he shouted "Cut" to the pilot, my heart was in my mouth, but, even though I was petrified, there was no way I could let my younger brothers see my fear.

So, with a steely look in my eyes, I manoeuvred into position, facing forward with both legs out. It was only 2,500 ft or about 800 m, but I can assure you, it was petrifying to me.

I could write a page or two explaining the exact procedure, but I won't bore you with it.

When my canopy opened, the beautiful view and feelings were truly amazing.

When all three of us had landed, gathered up the canopy and returned to the centre, we all agreed to jump again.

It must have been about an hour or so that we were all getting into the cramped "Islander", then 20 mins climbing to altitude and preparing to jump.

At this point, I was crapping myself, thinking, why the heck was I doing this again.

Actually, after my second jump, although it frightened the life out of me, I knew I was going to do a lot more.

On occasions, we, the bunch of skydivers, were always looking for what most people would think of as "stupid" things to do that would get our hearts racing. On one particular weekend, one person suggested that a group of us would do a night naked jump off the bridge into the river Nene in the nearby village.

On this occasion, I think about 20 of us drove down. We all stripped off on the little pathway beside the bridge, and then when there was no traffic, a group of us would run up on the bridge, holding hands, and jump off into the water fifteen or twenty feet below. One of my mates, Dennis Jones, slipped as he was running back along the path. We all tried not to laugh as we saw that our wet, naked friend had fallen into a bunch of nettles.

Not funny to him, obviously, but trying not to laugh as we dragged him out of the nettles was nigh on impossible.

Zephyrhills...

As my life associated with what now was not basic parachuting but real Skydiving, things changed a lot in my attitude to life and general demeanour. I think jumping out of an aircraft from over two miles high certainly puts a different perspective on how you see things.

My Life-85

Although this was mainly a weekend visit to Sibson twice monthly, I'd now done over 500 jumps, mainly with the team I'd formed, consisting of me and three good mates.

We competed in various competitions, including the British Championships (The Brits). If I remember correctly, the best we'd done was finishing 7th, and no, there weren't only 8 teams.

Something all skydivers at that time dreamt of doing was being able to spend a couple of weeks at Zephyrhills in Florida.

So many of the greatest skydivers in the world had spent weeks, months or even years either just jumping or actually working as an instructor.

I was lucky enough to go on three occasions, once with my team to prepare for "The Brits" and twice just with friends who enjoy the weather, etc.

My Life-86

On one occasion, I was one of 40 skydivers crammed into a DC3.. (forty tango) that, after climbing to an altitude of 17,500', circled Cape Canaveral, then watched the Space Shuttle take off and fly only 3 miles away. We were able to watch until the fuel pods were jettisoned, I was one of seven jammed into the door, an amazing sight, truly amazing.

Guinness Book of Records

If I remember correctly, it was in 1989 that I was extremely lucky to be part of the British record attempt to have sixty skydivers in specific positions to form a 60-way.

The record at that time was 45. You have to understand that skydiving was truly in its infancy, so the 45-way was good, and the 60-way, at that time in the UK, had never been achieved.

I was part of the 6 man base format that all the others docked onto; as I said, everyone had a very specific place, so you couldn't just latch on anywhere.

In order for it to be verified, it was filmed from the ground and by three cameramen in the air. We completed the 60 way on our 3rd attempt, so YAY !!! I was in the 1989 Guinness Book of Records.

My life with Juliet was getting more and more difficult, and as I said, my infidelity just happened. At the end of the day, regardless of justification, I was wrong to do it. When a couple makes the commitment to marry and be faithful, that's what should be done.

So we divorced. Josh was only 11 months old, but I felt that for him to grow up without witnessing his parents constantly arguing would be better for him and his sister, Lucy.

Number two.

Six years after my divorce, I met Debbie, who I thought was my forever wife; four years later, after her numerous affairs, we separated, and we tried getting back together; at the time, I had been living in Florida and successfully trading on the NASDAQ, but, no that didn't work, and my second divorce was finalised.

Looking back, I can genuinely see that I and most of the other skydivers had a very different, almost carefree attitude and constantly challenged and dared each other to do ridiculous and stupid things, ignoring the obvious dangers, but that was "Life".

Chapter 9: Florida

After the experiences of my stupid and selfish infidelity, my two kids by my first of two wives, and the constant driving for work, which was in excess of 50,000 miles per year, I decided to use my experience to go alone.

I'd been divorced from my first and second wives and was now living in a rented room in Norwich.

Please remember that back then, in the late 90s, the Internet was still very new to most people, and in the very rural area of Norfolk, it was almost unheard of, but I was and am a very optimistic person and thought I could bring this new technology into the lives of the everyday person.

After a year of trying, the dot com company I'd created, www.only4norwich.com, failed to provide a justifiable income for myself, so it was back to the drawing board.

I have to explain that in addition to my skydiving experiences, I'd also trained successfully as a SCUBA diver; it's written in caps because its Self Contained Underwater Breathing Apparatus.

I had an idea to go to the USA to learn to be a pilot. Once I'd done that, then many doors would open, and there was even the possibility of getting my Jet Commercial license and flying for an airline, which is difficult and expensive, I know, but possible.

Anyway, after a considerable period of time involved in research, back in the days before the numerous search engines of today, all research was done via books, magazines and the trusted but expensive telephone. I learnt about a flying school in Flagler Beach, which is about 20 miles north of Daytona Beach and about 40 miles south of St Augustine on the east coast of Florida.

The PPL course included accommodation, although I was later to realise that accommodation meant bunkbeds in a tiny and cramped room shared by three others that were also learning to fly. Being in this claustrophobic environment was very uncomfortable and inconvenient. The owner of the house was a Scottish woman with two dogs that insisted on clawing themselves along using their front legs and dragging their butt's on the carpet to relieve an itch (worms).

So I understandably moved to a great place on AIA, the main road that ran alongside and right between the house and the ocean.

Jack and his wife Anne ran the place, although, at the time, Anne was sick and bedbound, so it was only Jack that I dealt with. He was a great guy. He always spoke in a very loud voice. I realised that he spoke loudly because his wife couldn't hear him when he talked normally, so I just accepted it as perfectly acceptable.

Jack's dog, one of the Heinz 57 varieties, was huge but relatively docile at home.

To help out on occasions, I took the dog, which Jack had named "Boy". Yes, I know it was strange, but it was what it was, for walks on the beach. Not surprisingly, when "Boy" was on these walks, Ha !!! Not so much walks but drags because "Boy" took advantage of the fact he was out with the far more lenient me and on the beach, not the hard pavement. So he would drag me for hundreds of yards, regardless of my constant shouts for him to stop; on one occasion, he actually pulled so hard that I actually tripped and fell headlong onto the sand. I think it was only his tiredness from dragging me that made him stop.

I remember Jack laughing loudly when he saw my clothes and hair covered in sand. It was after his belly laughs that Jack explained why he only walked "Boy" on the sidewalk.

At this time, I'd taken and passed my private pilot's licence or PPL in only 43 hours; the minimum is 40 hours, and the national average in America is 75 hours.

It was in 1999 that I'd rented a Condo in St Augustine, a beautiful town about 40 miles south of Jacksonville,

I had many wonderful memories of my time there, but it was also the beginning of such a detrimental and life-changing experience.

One day, after returning from my visits to the gym and the supermarket Wynn Dixie, I was carrying bags from each and walking up to the top floor of my Condo.

Three steps from the top, my foot tripped, and with no free hands to break my fall, it was my face, my mouth specifically, that smashed into the top step. On opening my eyes, all I saw were teeth and blood.

Obvious dental visits followed, I think it was three, where extractions and root canals were what I mistakenly thought my saviour.

My time in Florida was limited to seven or eight visits of 90 days each, as I was a Non-Resident

Alien at that time. I'm reasonably confident that my final visit was in 2001.

I was very lucky in that my mum, R.I.P., very kindly helped me financially to have the very expensive dental work. Obviously, at that time, the cost of living in a Condo on the beach, renting a nice car and simply supporting myself took thousands every month, but I managed this through a reasonably successful career trading on the NASDAQ during the dot com boom, sadly that came to an end when I made a couple of bad investments that resulted in me returning to the UK.

Fortunately for me, I was able to stay with Mum and George, her third husband, who, in reality, was loved by everyone in our family.

Over the next year or so, I continued with my dream of trading on the stock market. I initially thought that things were going great, but one of my brothers, who was unbeknownst to me, was a very sneeky liar who ruined the lives of many people, including family and people who mistakenly thought of him as a friend.

What really upset me, not so much at the time, but as the months and years went by, I'd succumbed to my brother's lies and not shared the truth with my siblings and even more so with mum and George, so instead of them knowing what a total shitbag he was, I'd gone along with his lies and let my brothers and sisters believe that it was just bad luck when we all lost a considerable sum of money.

What sickened me was realising years later that when we'd all put significant sums into his pockets, believing the full amount was to secure the shares, but finding out that only half of the thousands we'd paid was to buy the shares, meaning he'd pocketed multiple thousands, but making us all believe that he too had lost money, he then perpetuated the lies by making the others think it was me, not him.

Anyway, I've far too much to be grateful for to let the actions of a selfish brother dominate my thoughts or the positivity I feel for me and my life, so.... see ya.

So, looking at my life and what I'd seen and experienced to date, I genuinely felt optimistic about what the future held for me. So when I'd had several two-hour telephone conversations with an American woman in Colorado called Dona, her stepmother's name was Donna, so her family all agreed to differentiate by spelling one Donna and the other, my girl... Dona.

My Life-98

As I said, it seemed that every day I was having a two-hour telephone call, which was great as we seemed to get along really well, but even though I was having the calls at 2.00 in the afternoon or 7.00 am for Dona, it was still very expensive, so when she suggested that I go over to Colorado to see her, it only took a few seconds for me to agree and make arrangements to fly over.

I'd never been to Colorado before, but to go to see the Rocky mountains and Dona, of course, really excited me.

I made arrangements and managed to get a flight in only two weeks. My heart was thumping in my chest; this could be a life-changing adventure.

Part Two

Chapter 10: America

I'm reasonably confident that if I chose to, then the Colorado section could genuinely be a separate book in its own right.

The things I did and the amazing people I met have made me a very proud man.

I hope I can instil the pride that I feel in my readers.

America...

On this particular day, February 2nd 2002, I'd got a lift to Heathrow and, with only one large bag full of important clothes, readied myself emotionally to meet Dona and prepare for what could potentially be a life-changing experience.

I remember meeting Dona for the first time at Denver Airport. I kept telling myself that even though she wasn't what I thought of as an attractive woman, we had got on fantastically over the phone, so I just told myself that looks didn't matter. It was character and personality that were the most important thing.

She wasn't ugly; she just wasn't pretty or not the physically attractive type I'd normally go for, but as I said, it was personality and intelligence that mattered. I had to ensure that the woman I'd fallen in love with on the phone was the same woman I'd flown over 5,000 miles to meet.

Colorado...

I think that the very first thing I noticed was that it was freaking cold. Okay, yes, Denver is at the foot of the Rockies and 5,280 ft above sea level, but for some reason, seeing the deep snow in places and the icy roads sort of shocked me, well not

My Life-102

really shocked, but made me see things differently than as I'd done in Florida where I'd been to many times.

Anyway, Dona seemed very happy and enthusiastic to meet me. She lived in a district called "Highlands Ranch", about 30 miles from the airport. Her house was a big 4 bed with a double and single garage overlooking the 9th green of a golf course.

She was a graphic designer and had her own business, and in all honesty, was quite successful, so it seemed obvious to me that, yes, she was reasonably successful and had a lovely house, mortgaged obviously, but she appeared to be the same intelligent woman that I'd had talked with on the phone.

So, my first impressions of her were positive. At the end of the day, in my view, it was far more important that we could just sit and talk and feel comfortable. It wasn't just about a physical attraction and wanting to be passionate and intimate.

Highlands Ranch...

It was a very nice suburb on the outskirts of what was considered as Denver Metro; back in 2002, when I moved there, the houses all varied in price from about $250k to $500k. Our house was about mid-range as far as cost was concerned, so getting a good and well-paid job was extremely important to me, although it didn't appear to be a priority as far as Dona was concerned.

During the following two years, I'd had jobs that were in the areas I was accustomed to, as in I.T.

and printing, although I did work for ADT in the newly formed Fire Systems Group, specialising in warning systems for smoke and fire, etc, in larger businesses, so I had to have specialist training to qualify me in a very unique field of business.

However, although the job paid reasonably well, I felt as if I was just marking time; yes, the money was good, but it wasn't fulfilling; it was just "a job", so I started looking for something that could provide a little more mental stimulation, as it happened I came across a position in the Asset Management and Tool tracking software industry which very much appealed to me.

It was in February of 2004 that I was diagnosed with what the medical world considers to be an incurable disease, multiple sclerosis, which, as I'm sure you can understand, changed everything in my life.

The two almost three years I worked there were definitely challenging in a variety of ways. I'd even been to New York to attend a trade show held by one of my biggest customers, which proved to be extremely beneficial for my employer and me, but again, I was getting the feeling that I was destined to be truly involved in helping needy people not just improving the profitability of financially huge organisations, which I had been doing.

Life-changing opportunity.

Although I wasn't looking per sè, I was told about a job through a work colleague who was suffering from an illness. His wife had been looking at possibilities of improving his health, and she inadvertently heard about a company that was involved in complementary medicine.

As I said, I wasn't looking, but after extensive research into who they were and what they did, I just knew that I had to call them.

I felt a little apprehensive to be calling a company like this; from what I'd read, they seemed to be a specialist organisation that was amazingly improving the lives of people who had genuinely been given no hope by traditional doctors.

There hadn't been a notification that they were looking for a new person in sales, but I felt compelled to talk to them. After speaking with the receptionist, I was put through to the senior manager, which surprised me but also made me feel good.

Maybe it was because my accent made me sound important; obviously, being an English man in the USA was different to the majority of locals;

My Life-107

anyway, I had a long conversation and was invited to come for an interview with the main man, Dr Huggins, next week.

I can't emphasise how excited I felt to have actually got an interview with the man who was truly saving lives. On the day of the interview, I wore my best suit and made sure my shoes were well-polished. Colorado is very much a laid-back state, so arriving at the interview looking so smart and well-dressed must have made a good impression on both the manager I'd previously spoken with and in my 90-minute interview with Dr Huggins because I was offered a job there and then. Doc, as I was informed how to address him, the manager spent a few minutes talking privately, then told me that it wasn't the job of a salesman they wanted me for. It was as the Client service director. If I said I was shocked, it would be an understatement, I was blown away and immediately accepted.

It was obvious to me that although the job of being a senior director with this company was going to be extremely demanding in more ways than a position such as this would normally have been. Doc was a world-respected professional in his specialised field. I could never hold a light to this man, but I needed to be professionally educated in his area of expertise.

During my years with Doc, I read everything he wrote and sat in on over 100 consultations, in addition to the days and weeks of study that were deemed necessary. Although it was never planned, as such, I also witnessed several hours of intricate dental surgery with two or three specialists who had been trained in his technique.

Only a month after joining, I attended a specialist seminar being held in Phoenix, Arizona. The four-star hotel was beautiful; I think that the fact that it was such a huge complex, with every amenity the guests could possibly want, and that it just seemed to be "there", especially as it was outside of the city and surrounded by desert. Not only was I able to sit in on the two weeks of intense training, but I also met several incredible doctors, dentists, PhDs and scientists wanting to expand their already extensive knowledge, which definitely helped me significantly in my quest as a knowledgeable addition to Doc and his efforts to help mankind. I'm sure that there are some people who might presume that my description of his work is exaggerated, but please trust me, it isn't!!!

Being present and able to see and hear several of the guest speakers, who, in their own right, were highly qualified academics with their own surgeries or laboratories, not only in this country but also in Europe in what is a much-unappreciated area of expertise, made me feel very humble, lucky and privileged.

There must have been in excess of fifty medical and dental practitioners attending, and to see the shocked look on the faces of these traditionally trained people was quite frightening. One fact that seemed to make the faces of several people change from just being sceptical to one of, "OMG, what have I been doing?" was when the statement about amalgam fillings was made. An amalgam filling which is placed in millions, literally, of teeth every year is made up of 52% mercury, with zinc, copper, tin and maybe 8% or 10% silver. Now, I know that so many people will recall that strange, almost unique sound they heard when the qualified and trusted dentist was pressing this into a tooth. But do you think that the patient or practitioner was aware that mercury is the most toxic non-radioactive substance on earth? No, I don't think so. Another fact is how many people grind their teeth, not every day, but often and for what seems to them to be for no apparent reason. Okay, let me shed some light on this: the several dissimilar metals making up the amalgam, as I previously said, combined will act as a receiver of radio waves, so when in certain environments, your teeth will be "buzzing" in your jaw, the natural thing for any person to do, is to grind your teeth together which is like twiddling the dial on the old radios to change channel's, and distorting the signal and stopping the need to continuously grind your teeth. As I said, the look on people's faces and the 'Oh" expression was quite honestly something I'll never forget.

My Life-112

The weekend seminar was extremely beneficial, not just for me but also for the attendees, some of whom had travelled thousands of miles and at great expense, but to have experienced first-hand information from Doc and the other speakers would play an integral part in helping people was priceless.

Texas...

At a clinic a couple of years later in Texas, I physically met a man and his carer, who was his wife. We had talked on the phone on numerous occasions after he'd heard of the genuine possibility of restoring his health. He, like many others, had been informed that the disease he'd been diagnosed with was incurable. What I learned over the years of study with the doc was that the diagnosis of incurable, not in every case obviously, but many, incurable, should really be termed as not financially viable to be "Cured" by big pharma.

Anyway, the first of the two-week clinics were for the extensive dentistry that would be performed by one of the expertly trained dentists who could boast of intricate and precise training from Doc but also decades of traditional dentistry experience, then one week of Dr Huggins explaining the how, what and why's of what life in the future would require.

It was quite flattering for me to think that I had played a small part in the improvement of his life. I felt elated when, on the first day of the 2nd week, the doctor was to explain some of the detailed dental work that had been previously done by the other dentists. I sat at the front of the class alongside Dr Huggins as I would be speaking to them. This particular client, who had been having serious issues with mobility, came into the class and almost ran to me when I introduced myself. The hug he gave me made me want to cry with joy. He was a very successful businessman with factories in the US and Asia; he and his wife asked me if I'd like to come out to their New York house to attend a big party they would be having soon; apparently, they had several friends that they thought would like to meet "me", if I wasn't in a serious relationship, I would have gone, but the conscience I have, overruled my obvious attraction.

Over the next couple of years, I can genuinely state that the experience I gained and the people I met, some of whom started as clients or practitioners following in the practice and methods perfected by Doc, had later transitioned into friends that I had for many years, were very special to me.

Unlike any position I'd held in the past, regardless of the country I was in, it never affected me emotionally as much as my years with Dr Huggins.

Some people have experienced the most gut-wrenching health problems because some medical practitioners have done nothing more than prescribe drugs to ease the discomfort and pain of the disease they had been diagnosed with. When someone came to us as a last resort, maybe a friend or relative had read or heard that Dr Huggins could be an option. It may well have been too late to genuinely save their life; on a few occasions, I had to get away from the office and just sit in a tranquil mountainous area and cry like a baby.

In 2011, the company and Doc specifically were struggling under the constant pressure of "The powers that be", who had some serious financial connections; obviously, I can't name specific people or companies, but I'm sure you can work it out.

So, the doctor was forced to change and adjust his focus while still helping the uninformed public. So doc diversified and focused his research on DNA and body chemistry rebalancing. This requires specialists in this complex field; unfortunately for me, that wasn't what I was good at, so later that year, I was made redundant.

It's difficult to explain the sadness deep in my heart. Yes, financially, it hit me, but emotionally, I was devastated.

Chapter 11: England

Over the next year or so, I'd taken a couple of jobs back in the computer s/w industry, but as I said, unfortunately, these companies all seemed to be an hour away, up in Denver, so it was back to driving for an hour to get to work, all day at work and then another 60 or 75 minutes drive home.

I'm sure that the anxiety and emotional stress caused by this had an extremely negative effect on me and this hideous disease, which resulted in me making a commitment to return to England.

I'd decided this after a very bad episode of MS after a tough day at work, then feeling so negative, bordering on depression and long telephone conversations with one of my nieces and a sister. In all honesty, I genuinely think I had given up all hope and was so close to ending it. I truly never thought that suicide would be something I'd contemplate, but it did happen, and fortunately, they convinced me to come back to England after almost eleven years in Colorado and 2 1/2 in Florida.

It was weird to tell Shari who I used to work with, that she and her husband could come to my apartment in a few days and take any of my furniture, which was only a few months old.

I stayed with my elder sister Suzie between November and March until I moved into my flat in Worksop, about 20 miles from the little village where Suzie lived.

The flat/apartment was one of 10 in a purpose-built building on a main road. It was good in some ways but bad in others.

My flat had patio doors straight onto the garden, which was the good part, but they also looked out onto the main road, so traffic could be noisy on occasion, and twice each day, I listened to hundreds of teenagers going to or from school.

Good or bad was not an issue at this time. What did matter was me and my health and maintaining my focus on ridding my body of what traditional medicine perceived as an incurable disease.

The following two years were very much years of existing, not genuinely living, and please understand what I've said here; those years were bland, as in I felt as if my "life" as I'd known it to be simply didn't exist anymore, so instead of just giving up and accepting defeat to the life-sucking disease, I decided to genuinely attempt to achieve something that ever since knowing Dr Huggins and what he so painstakingly achieved, I decided to attempt to get my doctorate, once I'd made the commitment mentally and emotionally, I set about researching, which involved hours of Web searches and phone calls. Obviously, the Open University was going to be my best option, or so I thought, but as it happens, it's not a financially viable option for pensioners as paying almost £4,000 per year just wasn't possible even though I still had a little saving from my time in the states. Hmm, the States? I wonder!!!!

I had started my BA while working for Doc; maybe, just maybe, there was a possibility of resuming my two-plus years...

I genuinely felt weird back then in Colorado because it was done in secrecy from my colleagues and staff, but because Doc genuinely had so much to be wary of, it was kept between him and myself and the university, of course.

My Life-121

So, back to my inquisition, after at least six calls, it was agreed that I could be awarded an honorary degree on the basis that I would attempt to achieve a PhD. This was also done with an agreement to act in a supervisory role upon completion and returning to Colorado as I'd planned.

It required me to submit my research weekly and report to my supervisors via Zoom calls. They were WhatsApp and video calls during the initial three years of my eight-plus years of four hours of research daily spent achieving this.

I'm sure that some people would think that this could be seen as a ridiculous waste of time, money and energy, knowing that I am almost seventy years old. Wow... just saying and acknowledging my age makes me feel... strangely vulnerable. I'm 24 years older than my dad was when he sadly passed, then Uncle Ted didn't last that much longer, and I'm about fifteen years older than the passing of Uncle Jim (Fred), my elder brother Geoff made it to sixty, so it seems that the male members of the Cairns family aren't people that live long lives, but I just wanted to prove it to myself and achieve something never done by a family member, but I also knew that I would never use this qualification professionally, but from a personal point of view, the knowledge and experience of working so closely with Dr Huggins, in my opinion, was quite frankly, amazing. I wanted to be a part, albeit small, in perpetuating the incredible work he has done, so instead of being seen only as someone who worked for him, I wanted the personal satisfaction of knowing that I could do it.

Ann Boroch...

Anyway, back to 2018, as I previously said, my sister Suzie, who had done very well for herself, now lived in a lovely big house in a little village, a Hamlet really, and on her land, she also has 350 Yr old barn that she was having converted into a small cottage, which I could live in at a reduced rental cost in comparison to what she could justifiably charge.

So, with help, obviously, I moved in, which would mean that I'd have company every day and be able to have proper conversations instead of just deciding on my meals, etc.

One day, I found some research that quite honestly changed my life; it was an article about a 24 Yr old woman who had been diagnosed with MS, unlike 99.9% of others receiving the depressing "your life as you know it is over" news, she didn't just accept it, she searched and searched for genuine reasons, that's very significant and true possible answers. What truly sickens me is how the trillion-dollar giants will only look for and create drugs... not medicine, but addictive drugs that only address symptoms, or what is referred to as DMDs or disease-modifying drugs, that way big pharma generates an abundance of customers; yes, customers that will become dependant and addicted to the exorbitantly expensive drugs.

Over the following 4 plus years, Ann lived by only eating food and drinks that didn't exacerbate the symptoms of MS but assisted the blood and organs in her body to truly heal itself because, in reality, it's designed by whatever higher power that you believe in, to do exactly that. When the human body is not contaminated by the hundreds and thousands of totally unnatural chemically adulterated additives that do nothing good or helpful to your body but, instead, just appeal to the tastebuds, then the body will do all its natural functions that are necessary to heal itself.

So, as I'm sure you can understand, after reading this, I made the commitment to myself to live my life as Ann suggested

I made a comment on social media and was very pleasantly surprised when I received a response from an incredible woman who had actually spoken with Ann Boroch and had followed what I then learned was called the Ann Boroch Protocol or ABP for short.

I also learned that thousands of others, literally, had done the same, so, I was absolutely convinced and set about eliminating dairy, gluten and sugar. Now, I obviously am not making a statement or guarantee that this method will do anything, but I can say that the trillions of cells that exist to create the body are designed to function correctly when given the nutrition it needs.

I was already gluten intolerant and kept my sugar intake to no more than 4 or 5 grams per day, so completely eliminating sugar wouldn't be a problem. The issue for me would be dairy, as I love milk, cream and cheese, but I had promised myself that this was going to happen, and when I make a promise, I do it.

Because I'd joined this special group of people who had all made the commitment to change their diet to comply with "The Protocol", it meant that I was kept informed of the state, condition and progress of hundreds of others at that time, as well as being encouraged and motivated to persevere if ever I had doubts. Sadly, what is told to every sufferer of this hideous life-sucking disease is that there is no cure and that we have to mentally and emotionally prepare for what "they" consider to be inevitable. Personally, I can tell you that that is extremely depressing, especially for me, when you consider how physically active I've been.

But, as I said, I was now part of a group of people following a dietary program that had removed the damaging toxic foodstuffs, enabling the restoration of normal bodily functions.

Please understand what I'm saying; I'm not making a statement or guarantee about "curing" anything.... because there are many multi-billion pound organisations that have proven, from a financial standpoint, that creating a drug that actually "heals" is not a financially feasible practice, so is not available. But what I am saying is that by only giving the body the nutrition it needs, the internal organs can heal themselves.

In my previous job, I explained to hundreds of people that it's far better to attempt to correct the cause of the problem or health issue, not to simply address a symptom, which, as I said, is what the majority of pharmaceutical drugs do.

For example, if you came home and saw the kitchen floor was flooded with water, what "they" tell you to do is to get several towels to mop up the water, a never-ending job. What the ABP recommends is to turn the tap off, pull the plug out of the sink, and then mop up the water. Fix the Cause, not the symptom.

Again, I want to make this very clear: I am not... I am NOT advising or recommending or suggesting that anyone suffering from any disease do anything that I've personally done to almost completely eliminate the disease that I was diagnosed with, but if you did your own thorough research on DRUGS, I'm sure your findings would be similar to my own.

Weakness...

I was definitely noticing a big difference in the reduced MS symptoms I was now experiencing. I'd been religiously adhering to the dietary recommendations of the ABP. Knowing that not only was I feeling the difference, but I'd also talked on the phone to several people who confirmed very similar improvements, which obviously made me feel really good and confident about sharing this method with others who had genuinely been told that their life would only exist in as an MS sufferer, reliant on drugs that may well have eased some symptoms, but would possibly create others, notice that I've clearly said "possibly".

As far as my own MS symptoms were concerned, the only obvious symptom was and is an overall weakness throughout my body. However, that could logically be attributed to a lack of movement and general exercise. It did frustrate me somewhat. I mean, being physically active has always been a major part of my life. It was frustrating and humbling to be so restricted, but in my heart and mind, I knew that this was temporary, I am 100% confident that my strength would return.

I also have to point out that even though I'm not a "spring chicken" anymore, I'll be 70 years old next year. I'm still reasonably active on social media, and this has resulted in being in contact with several of the people who I'd met when I worked for Dr Huggins. Several people had contacted me simply because they wanted to stay in touch;

several clients of Doc may well have talked with me on numerous occasions during the years I was there. In all honesty, this made me feel good knowing that I'd obviously made a good impression on people who had attended the clinics in Texas or Pennsylvania for dental treatment with the dental specialists there, not Dr Huggins, who only explained his protocol.

Some of those people who had contacted me through the most popular social media had become friends, albeit telephone friends. But it still made me feel good and I enjoyed chatting or talking.

So, as everything about my health was improving, I was so positive and optimistic that I was moving around my house far easier than I had for six or seven years. One day that I remember very clearly as it was the same day that covid 19 was announced and everyone was advised to wear those ridiculous face masks, I'll comment about this later, but for now, it's not the main point.

As I said, I was getting around so much easier. Yes, I did have to rely on the walls and furniture to get around, but it was much easier. Anyway, I was in the bathroom and feeling really pleased with myself. I think I was a little overconfident and had a fall; my legs completely buckled beneath me and got trapped on either side of the toilet, meaning I was in excruciating pain with my hands and arms trying desperately to relieve the pain in my knees.

I live alone, and it was only about 10.30 am, meaning my carer wouldn't be here until 12.00. I can genuinely say that the pain was horrendous and constant. 90 minutes later, when my care worker came, I had to beg her to help. I understood they she wasn't qualified medically, but helping me to straighten my legs was, in my mind, of paramount importance. So I was now lying flat on the tiled bathroom floor, naked from my waist down, not that it bothered me; the paramedics arrived four and a half hours later.

After my vitals were checked and they could see no bones were broken, they efficiently lifted me into bed.

My thoughts were that I'd probably be confined to my bed for a couple of weeks, but I didn't take into consideration that the weakness in my legs would exacerbate so quickly. This problem was not going to go away, especially knowing that the care workers were not allowed to help me physically; this meant having to call and request help specifically from a physiotherapist, who obviously was not inclined to help an MS patient who didn't and wouldn't take the pharmaceutical drugs that only addressed symptoms.

My Life-134

As I'm sure you can imagine, this genuinely created a significant problem and was going to require me to be extremely diligent and focused on what I truly wanted, which was obviously to restore my health.

As I said earlier, in order to maintain my sanity and recognition of "life", I persevered with daily research, which, in turn, resulted in my desire to write at least 500 words daily, and in all honesty, I genuinely believe this to have played a significant part in healing myself.

On one occasion, I'd eaten food that upset my stomach really badly. I felt that it was food poisoning; maybe the meat hadn't been cooked enough, it wasn't done on purpose per sè but the care workers at the time, one specifically, had a bad attitude, she had no respect for my knowledge, experience and qualifications, she had that, "I know best" attitude of some 20 nothing-year-olds. I was really suffering from a serious gut ache, so my local GP arranged for me to be transferred to the nearby hospital. I was seen relatively quickly, but as expected, I had to sit alone in a curtained cubicle. Then, after a 9-hour wait, I was again transferred to a bigger hospital in Doncaster.

A doctor looked at my notes, and then I was installed into a ward of six; a cannula was inserted into my left arm, and an antibiotic was given every 8 hours. I wasn't happy about this, but there wasn't much I could do about it.

Obviously, the antibiotics helped, and the gut ache went away. I was seen again at about 9.30 am, and I explained my situation and opinion, which seemed to fall on deaf ears and be ignored. The doctor then announced that it might be gallstones, and if so, he would just remove the gall bladder

(Laparoscopy). He was shocked when I told him not object, but TOLD him that it was my gallbladder and it was staying inside me and if, if I had gallstones, then I would remove them painlessly and without an operation.

You can imagine the indignant look on his face; he only saw me on one more occasion when he agreed to discharge me and arrange to be sent home by ambulance.

It felt great to firstly not have the cannula in my arm and secondly to be back home in my own bed.

I know that while in the hospital, I got to see and hear lots of other voices, yes it was nice having different people to talk to, but just knowing that the medical staff were doing what they thought was best, I knew it wasn't, and I really disliked it when others were in control of everything in relation to my health. Yes, I know it was doctors and nurses, but they have been trained in the "treat a symptom" method, which isn't me.

The day after I got back, my sister popped in as usual. The difference on this occasion was that an argument broke out, well, not so much an argument but serious differences in her and my opinion.

Suzie is a lovely person and, in the main, would do whatever she could to help. The problem is that, in her opinion, she is right, regardless of who she's arguing with. Her opinion in her view is correct, and my opinion was wrong. I was accused of being stupid and uneducated. She also disrespected Dr Huggins, who, in mine and thousands of well-respected academic professionals, was an incredible man. Her insults and the "I'm so much more intelligent than you

" attitude just pushed me over the edge, and I made the decision to move out as soon as possible.

Over the next week, the council person that had been very helpful in the past recommended moving to a 48-flat building, specially for the over 60's in a small town about 25 miles away. He arranged for me to visit in the next week, which very much surprised but pleased me; it was great being outside in the fresh air.

I know it's not been easy or convenient for my blood relatives to actually physically help me or to come and see me, which most haven't, but if the roles had been reversed, I'm damn sure I'd have been a lot more considerate than some family members have been to me.

In the four-plus years I'd been there, I think I'd only been out of the house on 5 occasions, so how I'd stopped myself from going doolally amazes me.

Anyway, as I've previously said, keeping my mind active and researching a subject that, in my opinion, will be of genuine interest to others in the near future was of paramount importance to me.

Chapter 12: Overview

My life to date has been one of a great number of challenges and adventures. I've not succeeded at everything I've attempted, but I am proud of the fact that I've tried my best and lived by the rule of never giving up.

It was almost twenty-one years ago that I was diagnosed with what the neurologist told me was an incurable disease. I personally think and feel from what I've read about the two million plus people who have ever been diagnosed with this horrendous life-sucking disease that the majority simply accept what's been said. But not me; am I completely healed? No, but I can say that it hasn't beaten me.

I say my life to date because, yes, I'm 69 years old and obviously restricted because of my age and illness, but I'm confident in saying that you'd be hard-pressed to find a lot of people who have a greater and more varied collection of experience, and I can safely say that not only have there been many other "adventures", not listed here, but I can also say that the fat lady hasn't started singing, so, as they say.

It ain't over yet !!!

I am a proud man. I think some people, you know, the ones that just seem to have a defeatist attitude, would rather condemn my unwillingness to give up and accuse me of being stubborn. That may be the way other people see it, but as far as I'm concerned, giving up is never going to happen. The majority of people in the world can genuinely remark in a positive way on the fictional and historical characters in life that have succeeded against all odds: the Gladiators, Rocky Balboa, the Maggie Thatchers and Winston Churchill... I know that little old me, the scouser with multiple sclerosis, will never be a hero, but in my heart, I know it's me.

You can take the boy out of Liverpool, but you can never,

Take Liverpool out of the man...

Stefan Cairns

My Life-144

www.ingramcontent.com/pod-product-compliance
Lightning Source LLC
Chambersburg PA
CBHW051207120626
46547CB00013B/1237